THEMATIC UNIT
Shapes

Written by Jennifer Overend

Teacher Created Materials, Inc.
6421 Industry Way
Westminster, CA 92683
www.teachercreated.com
©2000 Teacher Created Materials, Inc.
Reprinted, 2001
Made in U.S.A.
ISBN-1-57690-615-9

Illustrated by
Blanca Apodoca

Edited by
Janet A. Hale, M.S. Ed.

Cover Art by
Denice Adorno

WITHDRAWN

Table of Contents

Introduction

Shapes is a captivating, comprehensive thematic unit. Its 80 exciting pages are filled with a wide variety of lesson ideas designed for use with primary children. At its core are three high-quality children's literature selections, *Brown Rabbit's Shape Book; Sea Shapes;* and *Pancakes, Crackers, and Pizza,* as well as a child-made mini-book. For these books, activities are included which set the stage for reading, encourage the enjoyment of the book, and extend the concepts gained. In addition, the theme is connected to the curriculum with activities in language arts, math, science, social studies, art, music, and movement. Many of these activities encourage cooperative learning. Suggestions and patterns for bulletin boards and unit-management tools are additional timesavers for the busy teacher. Furthermore, directions for child-created big books and culminating activities are included. This very complete teacher resource allows children to synthesize their knowledge in order to create products that can be shared beyond the classroom.

This thematic unit includes:

- ❑ **literature selections**—summaries of three children's books with related lessons (complete with reproducible pages) that cross the curriculum

- ❑ **poetry**—suggested selections for choral reciting

- ❑ **planning guides**—suggestions for sequencing lessons each day of the unit

- ❑ **bulletin-board ideas**—suggestions and plans for child-created and/or interactive bulletin boards

- ❑ **curriculum connections**—in language arts, math, social studies, art, music, and movement

- ❑ **group projects**—to foster cooperative learning

- ❑ **culminating activities**—which require children to synthesize their learning to produce a product or engage in an activity that can be shared with others

- ❑ **an annotated bibliography**—suggesting theme-appropriate literature

---

To keep this valuable resource intact so it can be used year after year, you may wish to punch holes in the pages and store them in a three-ring binder.

Introduction (cont.)

Why A Balanced Approach?

The strength of a balanced language approach is that it involves children in using all modes of communication—reading, writing, listening, illustrating, and doing. Communication skills are interconnected and integrated into lessons that emphasize the whole of language. Implicit in this approach is our knowledge that every whole—including individual words—is composed of parts, and directed study of those parts can help a child to master the whole. Experience and research tell us that regular attention to phonics, other word attack skills, spelling, etc., develops reading mastery, thereby fulfilling the unity of the whole language experience. The child is thus led to read, write, spell, speak, and listen confidently in response to a literature experience introduced by the teacher. In these ways, language skills grow rapidly, stimulated by direct practice, involvement, and interest in the topic.

Why Thematic Planning?

One very useful tool for implementing an integrated whole language program is thematic planning. By choosing a theme with a correlating literature selection for a unit of study, a teacher can plan activities throughout the day that lead to a cohesive, in-depth study of the topic. Children will be practicing and applying their skills in meaningful context. Consequently, they tend to learn and retain more. Both teachers and children will be freed from a day that is broken into unrelated segments of isolated drill and practice.

Why Cooperative Learning?

Besides academic skills and content, children need to learn social skills. No longer can this area of development be taken for granted. Children must learn to work cooperatively in groups in order to function well in modern society. Group activities should be a regular part of school life and teachers should consciously include social objectives as well as academic objectives in their planning. For example, a group working together to write a report may need to select a leader. The teacher should make this clear to the children and monitor the qualities of good leader-follower group interaction just as he/she would state and monitor the academic goals of the project.

Why Big Books?

An excellent cooperative, whole language activity is the production of big books. Groups of children, or the entire class, can apply language skills, content knowledge, and creativity to produce a big book that becomes a part of the classroom library to be read and reread. These books make excellent culminating projects for sharing beyond the classroom with parents, librarians, other classes, etc.

Why Journals?

Each day your children should have the opportunity to write in a journal. They may respond to a book or an event in their day, write about a personal experience, or answer a general "question of the day" posed by the teacher. The cumulative journal provides an excellent means of documenting writing progress.

Brown Rabbit's Shape Book

by Alan Baker

Summary

Brown Rabbit receives a beautifully wrapped gift. Inside the square box he finds a tube-shaped box with a round lid. Inside the tube he finds balloons in different shapes. Your children will enjoy identifying the shapes that Brown Rabbit finds.

Sample Plan

Lesson I

- Introduce or review the concepts of shapes (page 6, Setting the Stage, #2).
- Talk about giving and receiving gifts (page 6, Setting the Stage, #3).
- Read *Brown Rabbit's Shape Book* (page 6, Enjoying the Book, #1).
- Open a gift box (page 6, Enjoying the Book, #2).
- Complete Shapely Balloons (page 8).
- Participate in some Math Shape Up activities (page 43).
- Send home Parent Page (page 74).

Lesson II

- Read *Brown Rabbit's Shape Book* again.
- Make shape boxes (page 6, Enjoying the Book, #3).
- Learn a shape poem (page 35).
- Complete What's in Rabbit's Box? (page 9).
- Make a rabbit bed (page 6, Enjoying the Book, #5).
- Participate in more math activities (page 43).

Lesson III

- Complete Find the Rabbits (page 10).
- Play a mystery shape game (page 7, #1).
- Make shape headbands (page 7, #2).
- Blow circle bubbles (page 7, #3).
- Complete Shape Sets (page 46).
- Sing a shape song (page 68).

Lesson IV

- Complete Decorate the Gift (page 11).
- Make wrapping paper (page 7, #4).
- Practice gift-wrapping (page 7, #5).
- Play the Bean-Bag Shape Toss game (page 63).
- Sing another Shape Song (page 68).

Lesson V

- Make a shape book (page 7, #6).
- Play the Shape Spinner game (page 7, #7).
- Complete Shapes in Our Community (page 7, #8).
- Make a Shape Mobile (pages 64 and 65).
- Reread *Brown Rabbit's Shape Book* and make Rabbit Snacks (page 61).

Overview of Activities

Setting the Stage

1. Prepare your room for your shapes unit by displaying the interactive bulletin board: Can You Sort the Shapes? (page 71).

2. Ask the children to name the shapes they know. Draw each one on chart paper for all to see. Then introduce or re-teach the concept of squares, rectangles, circles, and triangles using the following activity: Create "shape tracers," which are simply cardboard cutouts of the desired shapes. Trace and cut out shapes from a variety of textured materials, such as sandpaper, felt, satin, cardboard, etc. Allow the children to touch the shapes as they say the names of each one. Draw the children's attention to the fact that the shapes may be different colors and they may feel different, but the name of the shape(s) remains the same. Next, collectively display all of the circles and have the children tell you the things that are the same and different about them. Continue in the same manner using squares, rectangles, and triangles.

3. Display *Brown Rabbit's Shape Book*. Tell the children that in this story Brown Rabbit receives a gift. Ask them to share stories about gifts they have received. Encourage further discussion by asking the following questions:

    • *When do people give and receive gifts?*
    • *Have you ever given someone a gift? What was it?*
    • *How do people wrap and decorate gifts?*
    • *What is one of the most favorite gifts you have received?*

Enjoying the Book

1. Read *Brown Rabbit's Shape Book* to your children. Encourage them to identify the shapes found in the illustrations.

2. Prepare for this activity by first placing several slightly inflated balloons in a tube-shaped oatmeal box. Place the lid on the tube and put it inside a larger box and gift wrap it. After reading the book, delight your children by displaying the gift box. Before unwrapping it, ask them to predict what they believe is inside of it.

3. Inside the story's gift box, Brown Rabbit found a box shaped like a tube. Provide each child with his/her own tube-shaped box (oatmeal canisters, cylindrical potato-chip cans, etc.) that has been filled with a variety of simple dye-cut shapes. Encourage the children to practice shape identification as they remove the shapes from their tubes.

4. Brown Rabbit blew up balloons and let them go. Show the children what happens when air is released from a balloon by blowing it up and, without tying a knot in the end, releasing the balloon. Watch it fly around the room! Now try the "balloon release" with a variety of different sizes and shapes (oval, round, elongated, etc.) of balloons. Ask your children to compare the way the released balloons flew around the room.

5. Your children can make their own rabbit bed boxes with this activity. Provide each child with a small box (such as a cigar or shoebox). Encourage the child to color or paint the box. To make a rabbit, the child needs to glue wiggle eyes and felt ears to a large cotton ball. Then place the rabbit in the box on a bed of crumpled facial tissue.

Overview of Activities *(cont.)*

Extending the Book

1. Brown Rabbit was surprised to find different shapes inside the box. Surprise your children with this "mystery shape" activity. Place a variety of different-shaped objects on a table. Place a tablecloth over the objects. Have the children use their hands to feel the shapes beneath the cloth. Ask them to tell you the shapes they felt and guess the identity of each one.

2. Have your children make decorative "shape" headbands. Using a 2-inch (5 cm) wide tagboard strip, measure the diameter of each child's head, allowing for a 1-inch (2.5 cm) overlap. Have the children glue different colored construction-paper shapes to their personal strip. Allow the glue to dry. Staple the ends together to complete the shapes headband.

3. Brown Rabbit made different shapes by blowing up balloons. Allow your children to make circles by blowing soap bubbles. Provide them with a mixture of liquid soap and water and bubble-blowing wands (available at most toy stores). As the children gently blow to make bubbles, encourage them to notice the different sizes, and possibly, shapes of the bubbles.

4. The wrapping paper on Brown Rabbit's gift was covered with shapes. Have your children make their own "shapely" wrapping paper. Provide a small section of bulletin board paper to each child. Have them use sponge shapes (available at most craft stores) dipped in different colors of tempera paint to decorate their paper. Staple the finished wrapping-paper sheets on a bulletin board or wall space to create an eye-catching display.

5. Wrapping gifts can be challenging, but fun. Create a wrapping center for your children to practice the skill of gift-wrapping. Provide empty square or rectangular boxes, pre-cut squares of wrapping paper (donated from home), and transparent tape. (If working with very young children, attach pre-cut strips of tape to the edge of a table for the children to use.) When they come to the wrapping center they can use the supplies to wrap a box. If desired, add ribbon for them to tie up their presents with a bow! As a culmination, have the children make a small gift and allow them to wrap it and give it to a family member or a friend.

6. Make a book of shapes. Duplicate pages 36–38 for each child. Cut the pages apart, stack them in sequence, and staple the pages together along the left edge. Read the shapes book with your children, identifying the shape of each character. Then allow them to color the pages.

7. Practice math skills using shapes by playing the Shape Spinner game on page 45. Duplicate, color, and cut out the spinner wheel. Glue the wheel to tagboard for durability. Attach a spinner by placing a brass fastener through one end of a paper clip. Press the fastener through the dot in the center of the wheel and spread the prongs to fasten it in place. To play, a child spins the paper clip and tells the name of the shape he or she has landed on.

8. Shapes are all around us. Encourage the children to look around the room to find shapes in the furniture and other objects. Distribute copies of pages 54–56. Have each child color and cut out the shapes at the bottom of each page. The children then determine where the shapes belong in the picture and glue them into place.

Ask $ to identify shapes in the objects they see

Shapely Balloons

Color the ◯s blue.

Color the △s green.

Color the ▢s red.

8

What's in Rabbit's Box?

Color the ⬜ s blue.

Color the ◯ s red.

Color the △ s yellow.

Color the ♡ s green.

Find the Rabbits

Color the rabbits brown. Color the rest of the picture.

Can you find ☐ s, ◯ s, and △ s?

    10

Decorate the Gift

Color the shapes. How many shapes are on the gift? _____

Sea Shapes

by Suse MacDonald

Summary

This book creatively displays a variety of shapes found in the ocean. Each double-page illustration focuses on a specific shape scene. The bold artwork features stars, circles, squares, hearts, diamonds, triangles, and more. The author also includes information in the back of the book pertaining to each of the highlighted sea creatures. This book is sure to inspire your children to become creative artists and use shapes to make a variety of sea creatures and scenes.

Sample Plan

Lesson I

- Participate in one or more of the pre-reading activities (page 13, Setting the Stage, #2 – #4).
- Read and discuss *Sea Shapes* (page 13, Enjoying the Book, #1).
- Participate in a shape walk (page 13, Enjoying the Book, #2).
- Participate in some of the Math Shape Up activities (page 43).

Lesson II

- Make a big book (page 39).
- Practice matching shapes (page 13, Enjoying the Book, #3).
- Make an ocean shape picture (page 13, Enjoying the Book, #4).
- Complete Find the Sea Shapes (page 18).
- Sing a shape song (page 68).

Lesson III

- Complete a shape graphing activity (page 14, #6).
- Use a mystery bag to help identify shapes (page 14, #1).

- Write a shape song (page 14, #3).
- Play a shapes concentration game (page 14, #4).
- Complete a shape chart (page 14, Extending the Book, #5).

Lesson IV

- Conduct or revisit some of the shape math activities (page 43).
- Make a tasty fish treat (page 62).
- Play Fishing for Shapes (page 63).
- Recite a shape poem (page 35).

Lesson V

- Complete Big Shapes, Small Shapes (page 34).
- Create and sing a class-created shape song (page 69).
- Reread *Sea Shapes*.
- Make Fishy Windsocks (pages 66 and 67).

Overview of Activities

Setting the Stage

1. Set the tone in your room by creating the bulletin board display: Ocean Shapes (page 71).

2. Ask your children to name all the different kinds of sea creatures they know. Write their responses on chart paper. Then display a variety of books with photographs of ocean animals in them. As new ones are discovered when you and your children browse through the books' photographs, add them to the brainstormed list of sea animals.

3. Create a learning center to generate interest in sea animals. On a table, display a variety of ocean books, as well as paper and crayons. Invite your children to view the books in their free time and then draw pictures of the interesting sea animals they find in the books. Post the completed artwork around the center area.

4. Ask children to think about the things they already know about the ocean. Using a large sheet of chart paper, draw a three-column KWL (Know, Want to Know, Learned) chart. Have the children dictate their thoughts to you. Record their responses in the first two columns. The final column will then be completed throughout the unit as the children learn new information about the ocean.

Enjoying the Book

1. Gather your children in a semi-circle on the floor so they can all see the book title. Spend a few minutes discussing the new book. Draw their attention to the cover. Have them find the title and the author's name. Ask them what ocean animals might be mentioned in the book. Tell them that each page features a different-shaped ocean animal.

2. Create an ocean-shaped walking path by first making large ocean shapes from construction paper (star for starfish, semi-circle for jellyfish, diamond for stingray, heart for fish, etc.). Arrange the cutout shapes in a path on the floor. Invite the children to walk the path, naming each shape as they go.

3. This activity will give your children the opportunity to match similar shapes. Duplicate the fish puzzle pieces (pages 15 and 16). Color, cut out, and laminate the pieces for durability. To assemble the fish puzzles, the children match a shape on the front half of a fish to the same shape on the back half of a fish. If desired, duplicate a set of fish puzzles for each child to take home for further practice.

4. Your children can create decorative ocean pictures using cutout shapes. Distribute a copy of the ocean background (page 17) for each child. Have them color it. Provide construction-paper cutouts of different shapes in assorted colors. Have them glue several shapes to the ocean background and then use crayons to add sea-creature details such as eyes, fins, and tails.

Overview of Activities (cont.)

Enjoying the Book (cont.)

5. Page 18 provides your children with the opportunity to identify shapes. Use this page to enhance children's knowledge of shapes by having them say the names of the shapes they find before coloring them.

6. The ocean graph on page 19 can be used in a variety of ways to provide your children with graphing experiences. Here is one suggestion: Display an enlarged version of the ocean graph. Label each column of the graph using different ocean animals found in *Sea Shapes*. Ask children to vote for their favorite ocean animal. Color squares to indicate their choices. Have them count the number of votes in each column; make mathematical comparisons with the numerical results.

Extending the Book

1. This activity adds a fun challenge to identifying shapes. In a paper bag, place several objects with very distinct geometric shapes. Gather the children in a circle to begin the game. To play, each child, in turn, reaches in the bag (without looking) and feels one of the objects in the bag. He or she then tells the group the shape of the object. Then he or she removes the object from the bag to reveal the shape. Continue in this manner until all children have had the opportunity to participate.

2. Your children will have fun creating shapes using a jumbo elastic loop. Create the loop by stitching the ends of an eight-foot length of stretchy elastic (available at most fabric stores) together. To participate in this activity, three or four children will need to step inside a created loop and pull the elastic up to their waist level. The children then collectively move to stretch the loop into a variety of geometric shapes.

3. The Write a Song activity (page 69) is a fun group-language experience. Copy the song outlines onto chart paper. Encourage the children to suggest appropriate words to complete each song.

4. This activity gives your children the experience of counting while continuing to practice their shape knowledge. Duplicate the shape and number cards (pages 47 and 48). Color, cut out, and laminate the cards for durability. Place the cards in a learning center or prepare a set of cards for each child. To play, a child arranges the cards face down in two rows (one row of shape cards and one row of number cards). The child turns over one card in each row. If the number of shapes on the card match the numeral card, the child keeps both cards. If they do not match, the cards are turned face down again. Play continues in this manner until all of the number and shape cards are matched.

5. Shapes are all around us and this activity encourages children to identify shapes in common objects. Duplicate the chart on page 57 for each child. Have him/her then cut out magazine pictures that resemble circles, squares, and triangles. Have the child glue the magazine pictures in the columns below the corresponding shapes on the chart.

14

Fish Puzzles

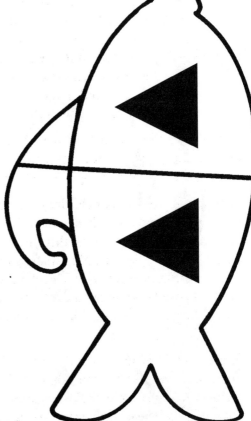

Fish Puzzles *(cont.)*

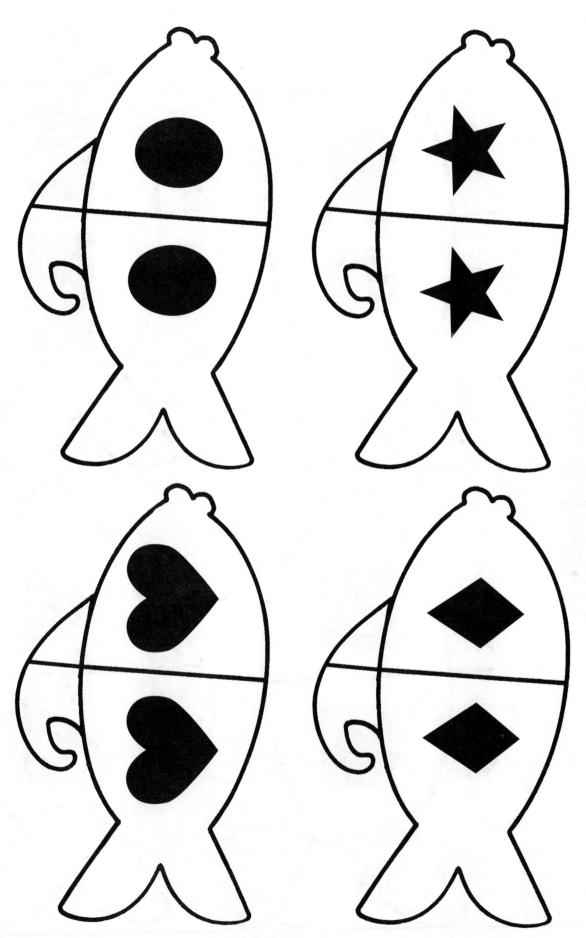

16

Ocean Shapes

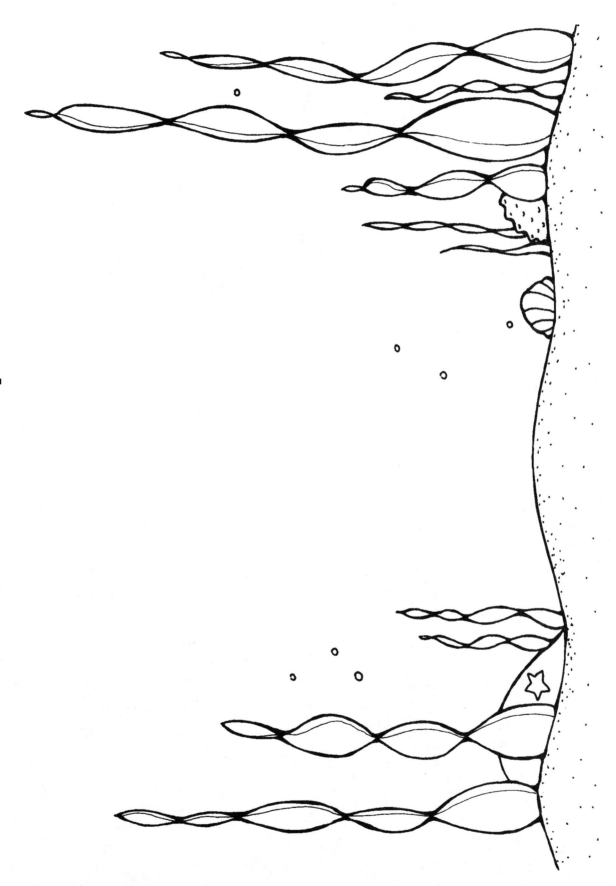

Find the Sea Shapes

Color the ⌓s red.

Color the ◇s blue.

Color the ♡s green.

Color the ☆s yellow.

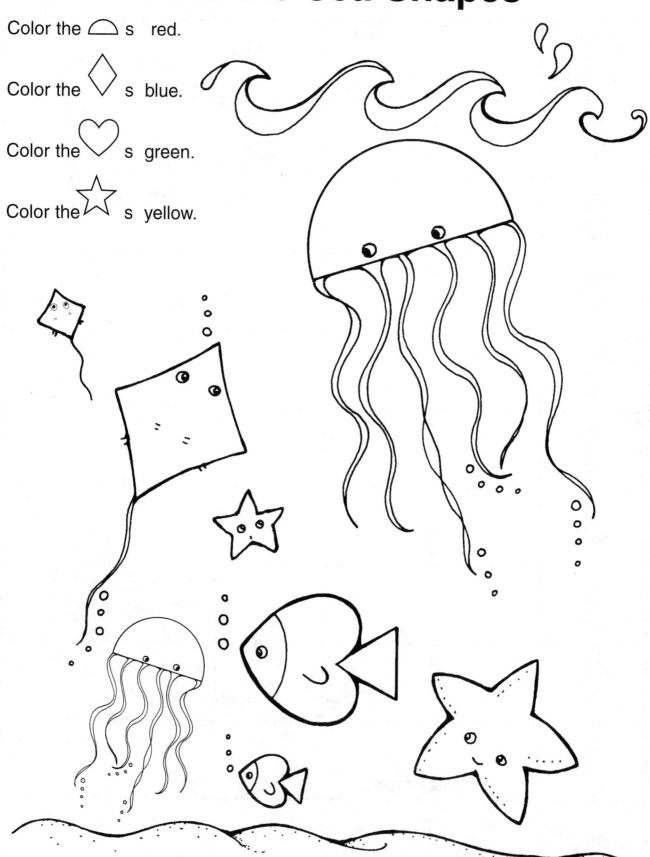

18

Ocean Graph

10					
9					
8					
7					
6					
5					
4					
3					
2					
1					

Pancakes, Crackers, and Pizza

by Marjorie Eberts and Margaret Gisler

Summary

Eddy loves to eat and eat and eat! He loves to eat foods that are different shapes. Eddy eats things that are round such as pancakes and eggs. He eats things that are square such as crackers and cheese. Your children will have fun identifying the shapes as they enjoy this book about a very hungry boy!

Sample Plan

Lesson I

- Conduct the interactive shapes bulletin-board activity (page 71).
- Discuss the shapes of foods (page 21, Setting the Stage, #2).
- Read *Pancakes, Crackers, and Pizza* (page 21, Enjoying the Book, #1).
- Participate in a cooking activity (page 21, Enjoying the Book, #2).
- Participate in some Math Shape Up activities (page 43).

Lesson II

- Read the book again.
- Make mini-books about favorite foods (page 21, #3).
- Learn a shape poem (page 35).
- Make a paper-plate pizza (page 21, #4).
- Complete Eddy's face (page 21, #5).

Lesson III

- Sing a shape song (page 68).
- Practice drawing shapes (page 22, #1).
- Make body shapes (page 22, #2).
- Participate in a picture-sorting activity (page 22, #3).
- Participate in more shape math activities (page 43).

Lesson IV

- Reread the book for a final time.
- Complete Food Shapes (page 22, #6).
- Participate in a table-setting activity (page 22, #4).
- Sing all of the the shape songs again (page 68).

Overview of Activities

Setting the Stage

1. Ask your children to think about the foods they eat. What shapes are they? Display a variety of foods, such as apples, tortilla chips, crackers, and cereal. Have the children name the shape of each food. Then ask them to think of other foods they enjoy eating and name those foods' shapes.

2. Display *Pancakes, Crackers, and Pizza*. Tell the children that this is a book about shapes. Encourage them to look at the cover illustration and tell you why this book is about shapes. Ask them the following questions:

   • *What is the shape of a pancake?*
   • *What shapes are crackers?*
   • *What is the shape of a whole pizza?*
   • *What is the shape of a slice of pizza?*
   • *What other shapes do you see in the illustration?*

Enjoying the Book

1. While reading *Pancakes, Crackers, and Pizza*, encourage your children to identify the shapes they see in the illustrations. Eddy has lots of food shapes on his table. What kinds of food shapes do we have on our plates for breakfast, lunch, and dinner?

2. After reading *Pancakes, Crackers, and Pizza*, your children are sure to be hungry! Using the recipes on pages 23 and 24, assist your children in making rice cake faces, crackers and cheese snacks, mini-pizzas, and/or cookie-cutter sandwiches. While making each shape snack, discuss the shapes of the ingredients used.

3. Have your children make booklets of their favorite foods. Provide each child with a booklet made from 9" x 7 ½" (23 cm x 19 cm) sheets of construction paper. On each page, have each child create and color a picture of a favorite [shaped] food and write a simple sentence to accompany it. For example, "I like apples. Apples are shaped like circles." If you are working with very young children, create pre-made pattern books using the template, "I like _____. _____ are shaped like _____.

4. There are many shapes associated with pizza. A whole pizza is round while a slice is triangular. There is also a variety of topping shapes. Have your children make their own paper-plate pizzas. Give each child a standard-size paper plate and a copy of the toppings (page 25). Have each child color the paper plate to look like a cheese pizza (crust [brown], tomato sauce [red], cheese [yellow]) and then color, cut out, and glue the toppings onto the pizza plate. Ask the children to tell you the names and shapes of the toppings.

5. At the end of *Pancakes, Crackers, and Pizza*, Eddy has circles for eyes, a square for a nose, and a triangle for a mouth. Have your children make Eddy's face by cutting and gluing the shapes found on page 26.

Overview of Activities *(cont.)*

Enjoying the Book *(cont.)*

6. Different foods come in a variety of shapes. Your children can classify shapes by completing Food Shapes (pages 27 and 28). Duplicate copies of these pages for each child. Have them complete the activity by cutting out the food shapes (page 28) and gluing them in the correct shape box (page 27).

Extending the Book

1. Your children can practice drawing shapes using copies of page 40. Before having them draw shapes on paper, provide a tactile experience. Fill a shallow pan with sand or salt and have each child practice finger drawing a variety of shapes.

2. Continue the practice of forming shapes with this class activity. Ask the children to stand and hold hands, creating a large circle. Draw the children's attention to the collective shape they have made with their bodies. Have the children move (still holding hands) to create other shapes, such as triangles and squares.

3. Other objects, besides food, have shapes. Encourage your children to visualize shapes in common objects by having them participate in a picture-sorting activity. Duplicate, color, and cut out the picture cards (pages 49–52). Laminate the picture cards for durability and place them in a learning center. To participate in the activity, a child categorizes the shapes by placing the circle pictures in one pile, the square pictures in another pile, and so on.

4. Teach your children how to set a table—while identifying shapes. Duplicate a copy of page 59 for each child. As the children look at the plate, napkin, and silverware draw their attention to the placement of each. Explain to them that the silverware and napkin are placed in specific locations beside the dinner plate, introducing the concept of "left" and "right." (If desired, create a learning center allowing the children to set a table complete with placemats, dishes, napkins, and silverware.) Continue the activity by cutting out and gluing food shapes (from magazines) onto the plate. Have each child tell the shape of each food as he or she glues it down.

Cooking Fun

Shape Face Creations

Ingredients

- large rice cake
- peanut butter
- round food items (such as banana slices and grapes)
- oval food items (such as almonds and raisins)
- square food items (such as cheese squares)
- triangular food items (such as apple wedges)

Utensils

- paper plate
- plastic knife

Directions

1. Place the rice cake on the paper plate.

2. Use the knife to spread a layer of peanut butter atop the rice cake.

3. Use at least one food item of each shape to create a funny face, by gently pressing each item into the peanut butter.

4. Let's eat!

Crackers and Cheese

Ingredients

- assorted shapes of crackers (circles, squares, triangles)
- cheese slices cut in circles, squares, and triangles

Directions

1. Provide each child with an assortment of crackers and cheese in various shapes.

2. Have them create cracker sandwiches by following verbal directions. For example, "Make a sandwich with two *triangle* crackers and one *round* cheese slice," or "Make a sandwich with two *square* crackers and one *triangle* cheese slice."

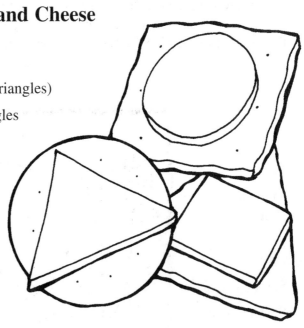

Cooking Fun *(cont.)*

English Muffin Pizza

Ingredients

- one English muffin half
- pizza sauce
- shredded Mozzarella cheese
- pizza toppings such as:

    black olive slices
    pepperoni slices
    mushroom slices

Utensils

- plastic spoon
- microwave oven

Directions

1. Spread a spoonful of pizza sauce atop the English muffin half.
2. Sprinkle Mozzarella cheese atop the sauce.
3. Arrange an assortment of toppings on the pizza. (Encourage the children to discuss the shape of each topping.)
4. Heat the pizza in a toaster oven or microwave until cheese melts.

Cookie-Cutter Sandwiches

Ingredients

- bread slices
- spreadable food items such as peanut butter, marshmallow cream, or jelly

Utensils

- spreading utensils
- cookie cutters (assorted geometric shapes)

Directions

1. Spread peanut butter, marshmallow cream, or jelly on a slice of bread.
2. Place another slice of bread atop the spread to make a sandwich.
3. Press a cookie cutter into the sandwich to make a shape sandwich.

Pizza Toppings

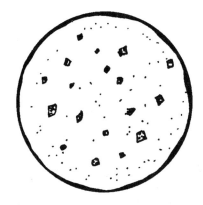
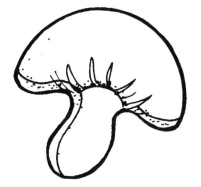

Eddy's Face

Cut and glue the shapes.

Food Shapes

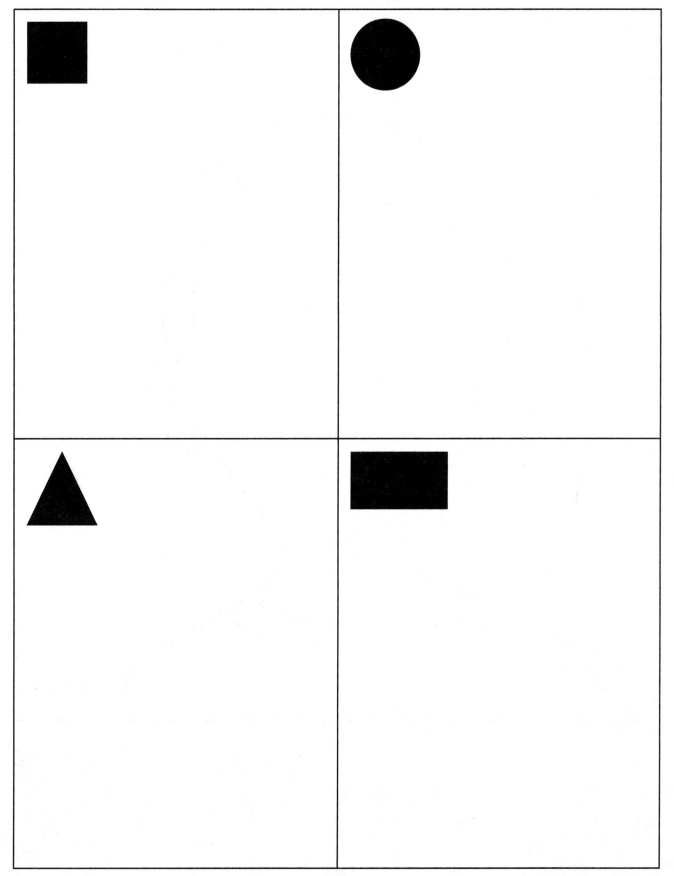

Food Shapes *(cont.)*

Shapes All Around

Summary

Make this mini-book with your children. Encourage them to identify the featured shape on each page.

Sample Plan

Lesson I

- Assemble the books (page 30, Setting the Stage, #1).

- Read *Shapes All Around*, discussing each page as it is being read (page 30, Enjoying the Book, #1).

- Search for shapes on your school grounds (page 30, Enjoying the Book, #2).

- Eat some Crackers and Cheese (page 23).

- Participate in one of the Math Shape Up activities (page 43).

Lesson II

- Reread *Shapes All Around*.

- Make shape finger puppets (page 30, Extending the Book, #1).

- Complete Shape Patterning (page 53).

- Recite a shape poem (page 35).

- Play Hide and Seek Shapes (page 63).

Lesson III

- Reread *Shapes All Around*; then read other shape books (page 30, Enjoying the Book, #3).

- Be a Shape Detective (page 30, Enjoying the Book, #4).

- Sing a shape song (page 68).

- Give the children a "hand" in identifying shapes in the classroom (page 30, Extending the Book, #2).

Lesson IV

- Review shapes using What Am I? (page 41).

- Enjoy A Shapely Celebration (page 70).

- Present children with Shape Awards (page 77).

Overview of Activities

Setting the Stage

1. Reproduce the mini-book pages (pages 31–33), one set per child. Explain to your children that they will be making their own books to color and take home. To assemble the book, cut the pages apart and stack them in sequence, aligning the left-side edges. Staple the booklet together along the left edge.

Enjoying the Book

1. Read the booklet to your children, pausing after each page has been read to allow them to identify the featured-shape objects for that page. Encourage the children to color the pages of the book after identifying all the shapes.

2. Give your children the opportunity to explore the school grounds looking for shapes. When they are outside, encourage them to look at doors, windows, playground equipment, plants, etc. to find different shapes. Ask them to tell you where they might want to look for specific shapes.

3. The Annotated Bibliography (pages 79 and 80) provides a list of shape books that you might like to read to your children or display in a classroom library.

4. Continue to encourage the identification of shapes in common objects by having your children complete the Shape Detective coloring sheet (page 60).

Extending the Book

1. Have some shapely fun by making finger puppets (page 42). Cut out the puppets and tape the tabs together to fit a child's fingers. Invite the children to engage in performances, pretending to be shape characters.

2. Let your children get their "hands" on the shapes in your classroom. Provide one copy of page 58 for each child. Have each child trace his or her own hand onto the paper in such a manner that the hand's fingers are spread out (see illustration). Have each child then cut out his/her hand and write his/her name in the center of the hand. As a class "listening" group, allow each child to verbally name a shape and locate a real object in the room that represents his/her named shape. Allow the child to then tape his/her hand to that named classroom object.

3. Shapes Online (pages 72 and 73) provides a list of Web sites for children, teachers, and parents, or utilize some Shapes Software (page 78).

4. Participating in the culminating activity on page 70 not only provides your children with fun learning experiences, but also gives them an opportunity to share their knowledge of shapes. Incorporate the activities listed, as well as others found throughout this book, and have a "shapely" time!

5. Present your children with Shape Awards (page 77) to honor their hard work in identifying, drawing, and working with shapes.

Shapes All Around

Name _____

Circles, circles here and there.
I see circles everywhere.

1

Squares are up and squares are down.

I see squares all over town.

2

Triangles are all around,

way up high, and on the ground.

3

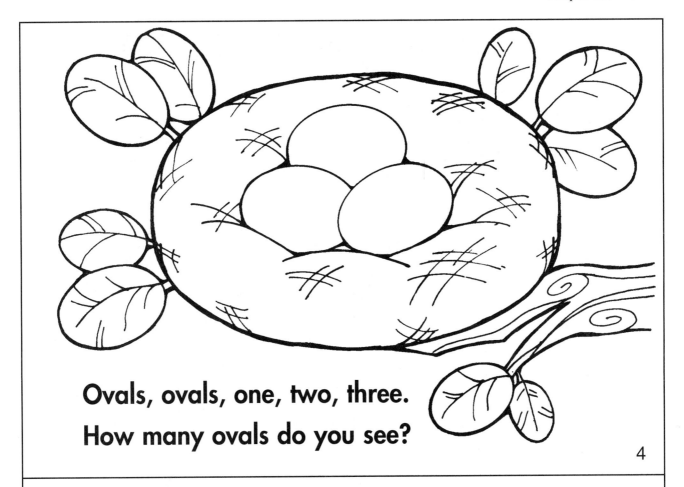

Ovals, ovals, one, two, three.
How many ovals do you see?

4

Shapes are here and shapes are there.
You can find shapes everywhere!

5

Big Shapes, Small Shapes

Make a ● on the biggest shape in each row.

Draw an **X** on the smallest shape in each row.

Shape Poetry

Shapes

Round and round and round we go.
A circle looks like a great big O.

Three straight sides and you'll see,
A triangle looks like a little teepee.

A box is here, a box is there.
Four straight lines make a square.

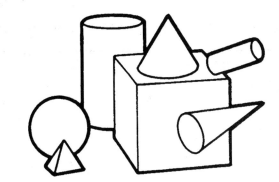

Shape Hunt

We're going on a shape hunt, a shape hunt, a shape hunt.
We're going on a shape hunt.
What shapes can you see?

Can you find a square, a square, a square?
Can you find a square?
Hold it if you dare.

Can you find an oval, an oval, an oval?
Can you find an oval?
Round and round.

Can you find a triangle, triangle, triangle?
Can you find a triangle
With three sides?

We're going on a shape hunt, a shape hunt, a shape hunt.
We're going on a shape hunt.
What shapes can you see?

Shapes Everywhere

Shapes on the table,
Shapes on the chair,
Shapes in the classroom,
Shapes everywhere.

Circles in the toy box,
Circles on the floor,
Circles in picture books,
Circles on the door.

Squares on the playground,
Squares in the hall,
Squares in the library,
Squares on the wall.

Shapes on the table,
Shapes on the chair,
Shapes in the classroom,
Shapes everywhere.

Shapes Booklet

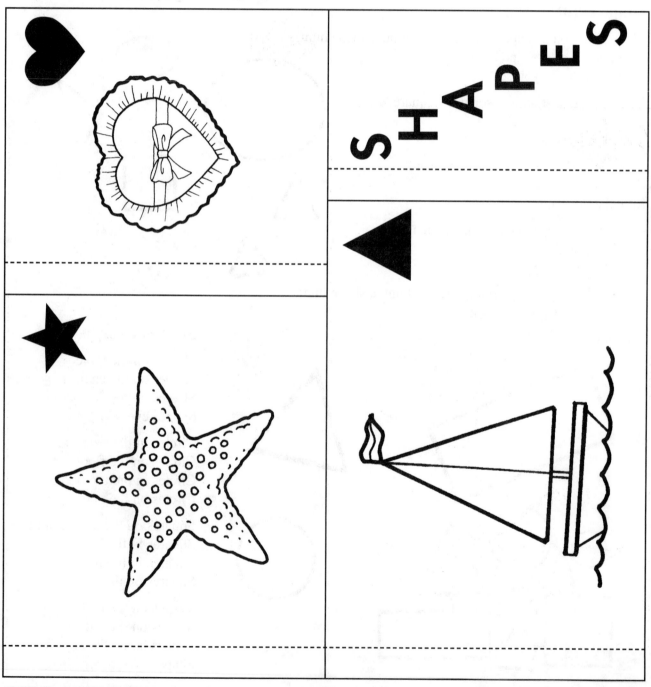

Shapes Booklet *(cont.)*

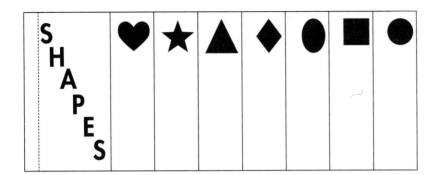

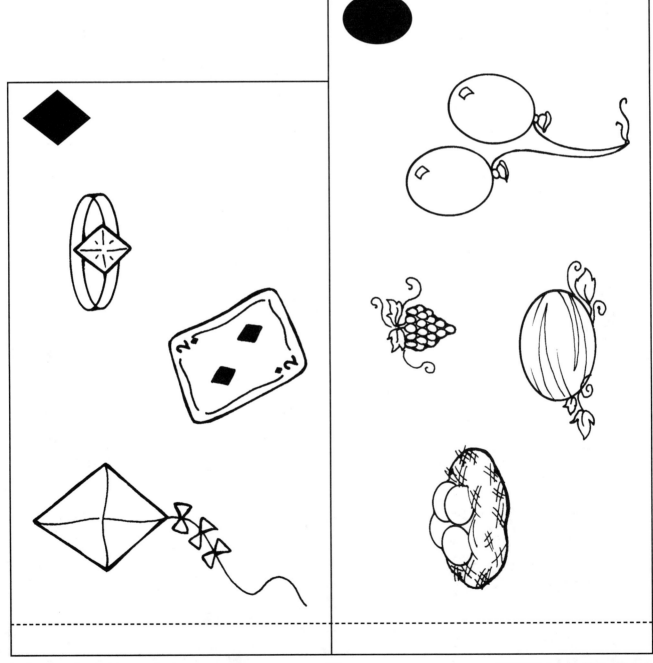

Shapes Booklet *(cont.)*

Making a Big Book

The making of a big book is a great cooperative activity for children. It allows them to combine language, reading, writing, and art.

Steps

1. Before making the big book, gather your children into one large group and review the shapes they have learned. Draw the shapes on chart paper and label each one (circle, square, triangle, oval, heart, etc.).

2. Divide the children into pairs. Provide each pair with a sheet of tagboard at least 12" x 18" (30 cm x 46 cm).

3. Assign each pair a shape to feature on their page. The two children then draw pictures of objects that have their assigned shape. Have the children label their pictures or write simple sentences describing their illustrations. (Young children can dictate their words or sentences to be written on the page by an adult.)

4. If desired, duplicate the shape patterns on pages 75 and 76 for children to also use on their pages.

5. When all groups' pages are finished, stack the pages in a desired sequence and top with a created title page. Staple along the left-side edge to form the big book's spine. (Optional Binding: If desired, create an accordion big book by laying each page on the floor with side edges touching. Place the title page to the far left. Connect the pages together by placing a strip of clear packaging tape where the side edges meet. Repeat the taping process on the backside of the pages for durability. Now fold the pages up accordion-style; display on a counter or tabletop.)

6. Read the book as a class and invite groups of children to read their pages to their classmates. Display the book for visitors to enjoy.

Drawing Shapes

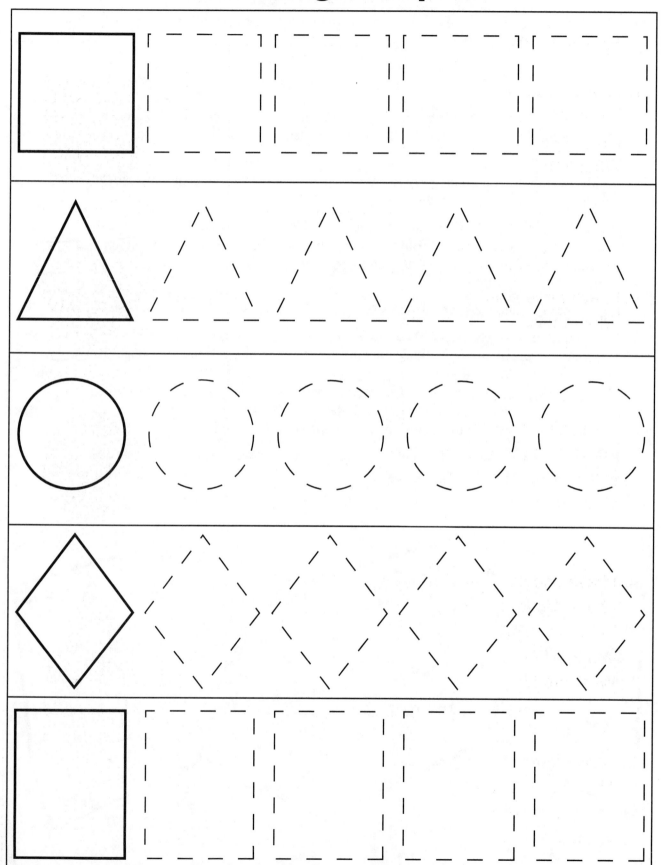

What Am I?

Cut and paste the shapes.

1. I have no points.
   I have no straight lines.
   I am round.
   What am I?

2. I have straight sides.
   I have three points.
   What am I?

3. I have four sides.
   I have four points.
   I look like a box.
   What am I?

4. I have one point.
   I have rounded sides.
   When you see me,
   you think of love.
   What am I?

5. I have four sides.
   My sides are straight.
   I am not a square.
   What am I?

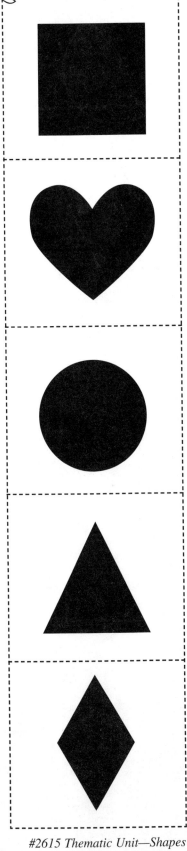

Finger Puppets

Math Shape Up

Copy Blocks

Your children can enjoy using building blocks with this copy-cat activity. Begin by building a simple structure using different shaped building blocks. Display the structure and encourage your children to copy it by building their own identical structure. As each block is used, have the child identify the shape. Extend this activity by duplicating the building-block patterns on page 44 for each child. Have each child color and cut out the blocks, identify the shapes, and glue them to construction paper to make artistic designs.

Copy Sticks

Prepare for this activity by making shape cards using wooden craft sticks. Glue the sticks onto construction-paper cards to form a square, a diamond, a triangle, and a star. To participate, a child selects a shape card and then uses a set of craft sticks to copy the shape. Have the child name the shapes when he or she is finished.

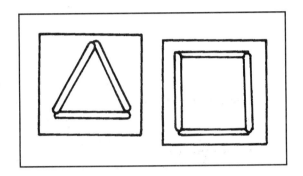

Button Sorting

Place an assortment of buttons at a learning center. Be sure to provide buttons in a variety of shapes. To participate, a child sorts the buttons into groups according to shape.

Shape Matching

This activity will help your children identify shapes. On a strip of tagboard, use a marker to draw seven different shapes (circle, square, triangle, oval, heart, star, and diamond). On each of seven clothespins, draw a corresponding shape. To play, a child clips a clothespin to the corresponding shape on the tagboard strip.

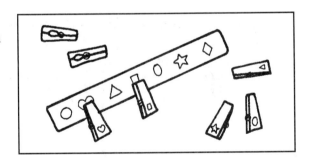

Circle Patterns

Place a supply of construction-paper circle cutouts in different colors in a learning center. Show the children that patterns can be made using different colored circles (red, blue, red, blue). Have them duplicate patterns created by you as well as create patterns of their own.

Shape Patterns

Place an assortment of construction-paper cutouts in a variety of shapes in a learning center. Display a shape pattern for the children to see (circle, triangle, heart, circle, triangle, heart). Have children continue the pattern and then create more shape patterns to share with classmates.

Pattern Blocks

Let your children manipulate, build, and play with pattern blocks. Encourage them to identify the shapes they recognize. Then have them tell the number of sides each shape has. Ask pairs of children to create imaginative structures with the blocks. When showing the structures to classmates, ask the children to name each block used.

Building-block Shapes

Shape Spinner

Shape Sets

How many in each set?

Shapes and Numbers Game

Shapes and Numbers Game (cont.)

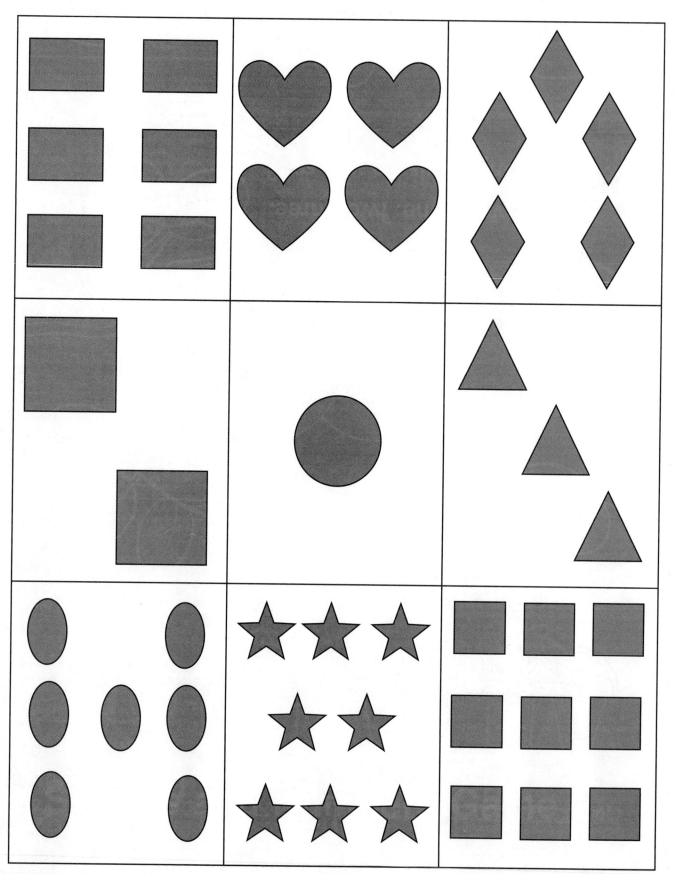

Picture Shapes

Picture Shapes *(cont.)*

Picture Shapes *(cont.)*

Picture Shapes *(cont.)*

Shape Patterning

Draw a shape to finish the pattern.

Shapes in Our Community

Can you match the shapes?

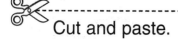 Cut and paste.

54

Shapes in Our Community *(cont.)*

Can you match the shapes?

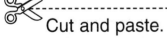 Cut and paste.

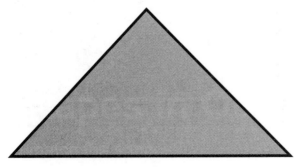

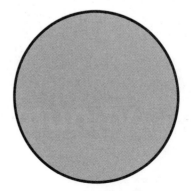

Shapes in Our Community *(cont.)*

Can you match the shapes?

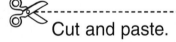 Cut and paste.

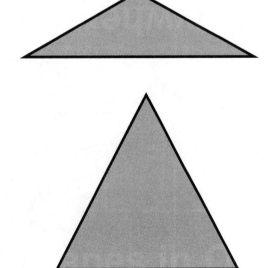

Shapes Are Everywhere

Shapes All Around Us

Trace your hand in the box. Cut out your hand shape.

58

Time for Dinner!

Shape Detective

Find and color these shapes: △, □, ◯, ▭.

Rabbit Snack

Ingredients *(per child)*

- one lettuce leaf, cleaned and dried
- two canned pear halves
- two banana slices
- three raisins
- four carrot or celery slivers

Utensils

- cutting board
- paring knife
- paper plate

Directions

1. Place the lettuce leaf on the paper plate. Top the leaf with one of the canned pear halves, hollow-side down.

2. Make the ears by cutting narrow sections, vertically, from the second pear half. Place near the narrow end of the first pear half.

3. Arrange the raisins on the first pear half to make the eyes and a nose.

4. Below the nose, place the two banana slices as shown.

5. Using the celery and carrot slivers, make the whiskers.

Extension Activities

1. While making the rabbit snack, ask the children to identify the shapes being used as the ingredients.

2. Use the leftover ingredients to make a fruit salad. Include additional fruit such as chopped apples, strawberries, and grapes in a large bowl. Pour orange juice over the fruits to moisten. Mix and serve.

Fish in the Ocean

Ingredients

- grapes
- purchased blue gelatin mix

Utensils

- knife
- bowl
- spoon

Directions

1. Cut the grapes in half, lengthwise.

2. Make the gelatin according to the package directions.

3. When gelatin is just starting to set (approximately one hour after chilling), fold in the grape "fish."

Additional Activities

- Make this recipe in a large glass bowl for a fish bowl effect, or divide up the gelatin mixture and place into individual cups or glasses before the gelatin sets.

- Make fish appear to be in ocean waves. After the gelatin has almost set, stir in one cup of whipped topping. Let the mixture set at least another hour before eating.

- A fun alternative is to use cheese fish crackers instead of grapes, although they are a little soggy when finally eaten (but children still seem to enjoy eating them!).

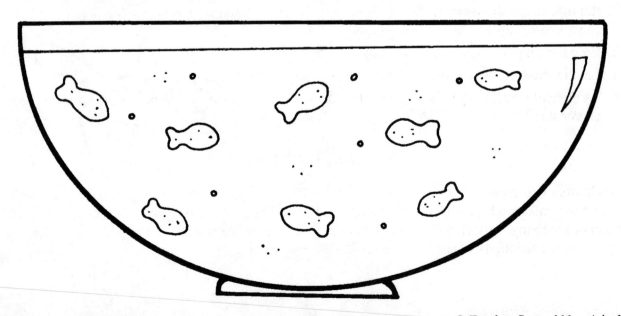

62

Shape Games

Bean-Bag Shape Toss

This lively game will help reinforce your children's shape-identification skills.

Materials

- one large, old bedsheet or large sheet of bulletin-board paper
- black marker
- an assortment of bean bags

Directions

1. Draw several large shapes on the bed sheet/sheet of paper to make a "shape mat."
2. To play, have each child, in turn, stand beside the shape mat holding a bean bag.
3. Call out a shape on the mat and have the child toss the bag onto that shape.
4. Continue in this manner until all your children have had the chance to participate.

Hide and Seek Shapes

Your children will enjoy playing this game of hide and seek while practicing shape identification.

Materials

- construction paper (assorted colors)
- shape patterns (pages 75 and 76)
- scissors
- pencil

Directions

1. Reproduce the shape patterns; cut out. Trace the shape patterns onto different colors of construction paper. Cut out the shapes.
2. Hide the shapes around the classroom.
3. Let the children search for the hidden shapes.
4. As the children find the shapes, have them identify them as they show their discoveries to their classmates.

Fishing for Shapes

Your children will enjoy fishing for shapes with this fun activity. Create a fishing pole by attaching a two-foot (61 cm) length of yarn or string to the end of a yard stick or dowel rod. Tie a small magnet to the end of the string. Attach a paper clip to each of several shape cut-outs. To play, a child fishes for a shape using the fishing pole and tells the name of the shape "caught."

Shape Mobile

Materials

- shape patterns (page 65)
- one sheet of 8¹/₂" x 11" (22 cm x 28 cm) tagboard
- scissors
- pencil
- construction paper (assorted colors)
- colored cellophane or tissue paper (optional)
- glue or tape
- hole punch
- yarn or string
- coat hangers

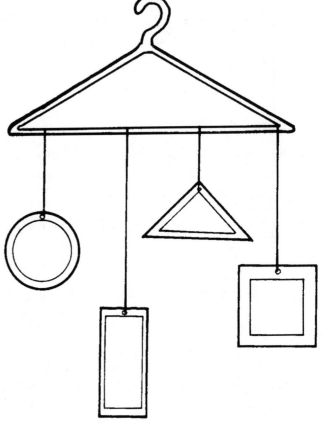

Directions

1. Reproduce the patterns onto the tagboard. Cut out the shapes.

2. Trace each shape onto a different color of construction paper; cut out each colored shape.

3. If desired, cut out cellophane or tissue paper to cover the hole in each shape cutout. Attach the cellophane or tissue paper to the shape's edges with transparent tape or a small amount of glue.

4. Punch a hole in the top of each shape and tie a length of yarn or string through it.

5. Tie the opposite end of the yarn or string to the coat hanger.

6. Suspend the mobiles from the ceiling for a decorative display.

Shape Mobile *(cont.)*

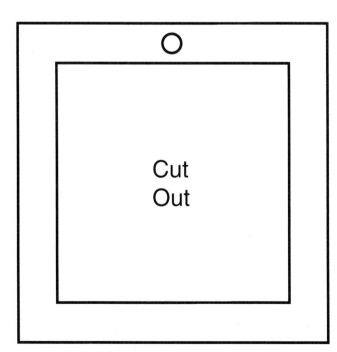

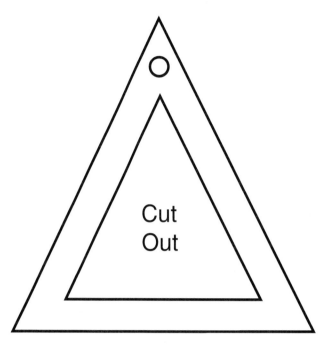

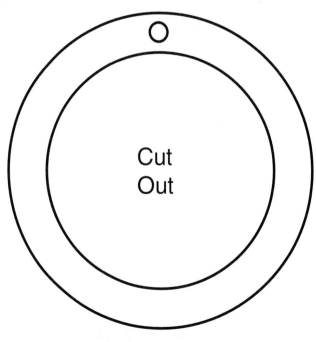

Fishy Windsock

Materials

- one 13" x 18" (32.5 cm x 46 cm) sheet of construction paper *(Sheet 1)*
- glue
- fish pattern (page 67)
- pencil
- one 9" x 13" (23 cm x 32.5 cm) sheet of colorful construction paper *(Sheet 2)*
- scissors
- crayons
- six 2-foot (61 cm) crepe-paper streamers
- hole punch
- yarn or string

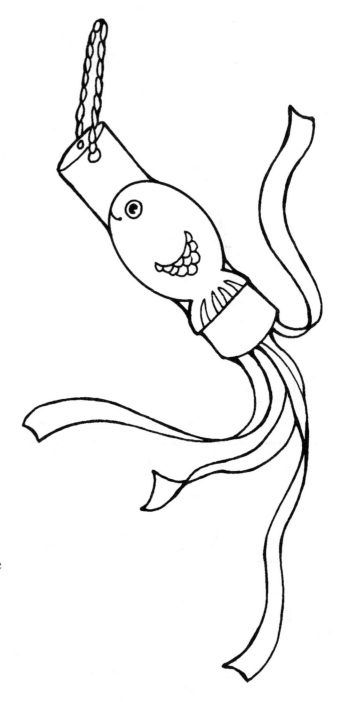

Directions

1. Glue the long ends of Sheet 1 together to make a tube.

2. Reproduce the fish pattern onto a sheet of colorful construction paper (Sheet 2); cut out and color using the crayons.

3. Glue the fish onto the tube; allow to dry.

4. Glue one end of each crepe-paper streamer to the inside of the tube as shown.

5. Use the hole punch to make two holes at the top of the tube (on opposite sides).

6. Tie the yarn or string through the holes to suspend the completed windsock.

66

Fishy Windsock *(cont.)*

Shape Songs

Shape Song

(Sung to the tune of *The Mickey Mouse Club* song)

Triangle, diamond, square, heart, oval, star,
All around, all around,
There are so many shapes that I can see.

I can draw all the shapes,
Aren't you proud of me?
Triangle, diamond, square, heart, oval, star.

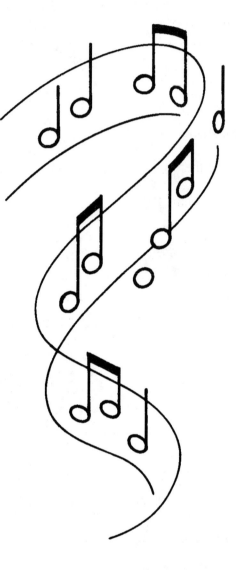

Have You Ever Seen...?

(Sung to the tune of *Have You Ever Seen a Lassie?*)

Have you ever seen a circle, a circle, a circle?
Have you ever seen a circle go round and round?

Have you ever seen a triangle, a triangle, a triangle?
Have you ever seen a triangle with three sides and points?

Have you ever seen a rectangle, a rectangle, a rectangle?
Have you ever seen a rectangle shaped like a box?

Have you ever seen a square, a square, a square?
Have you ever seen a square with four equal sides?

Have you ever seen an oval, an oval, an oval?
Have you ever seen an oval that's shaped like an egg?

Have you ever seen a shape, a shape, a shape?
Have you ever seen a shape? Tell me one right now!

Here We Go 'Round the Playground

Sing this song to your children as they go on a shape hunt around the school. The word playground can be changed to classroom, library, or other appropriate word.

(Sung to the tune of *Here We Go 'Round the Mulberry Bush*)

Here we go 'round the playground, the playground, the playground.
Here we go 'round the playground so early in the morning.

Can you see a circle, a square, or an oval?
Can you see a triangle so early in the morning?

Can you see a rectangle, a diamond, a star?
How many shapes can you see so early in the morning?

Here we go 'round the playground, the playground, the playground.
Here we go 'round the playground so early in the morning.

Write a Song

Choose a tune that your class knows well and change the words. Print the song patterns below (or use one of your own design) onto chart paper. Invite your children to contribute the needed words to complete each song.

(Sung to the tune of *Twinkle, Twinkle, Little Star*)

Shapes are _____ and shapes are _____.

I think shapes are really great.

I can see them _____.

I can see them _____.

Shapes are _____ and shapes are _____.

I think shapes are really great!

Example

Shapes are *short* and shapes are *long*.
I think shapes are really great.
I can see them *in the sky*.
I can see them *with my eye*.
Shapes are *round* and shapes are *flat*.
I think shapes are really great!

(Sung to the tune of *Mary Had a Little Lamb*)

I can draw a (color) _____, a (color) _____,

a (color) _____.

I can draw a (color) _____, using my (color) _____
crayon.

I can hold a (size) _____, a (size) _____,

a (size) _____.

I can hold a (size) _____, right here in my hands.

Example

I can draw a *red* balloon, a *red* balloon a *red* balloon.
I can draw a *red* balloon, using my *red* crayon.
I can hold a *big* beach ball, a *big* beach ball, a *big* beach ball.
I can hold a *big* beach ball, right here in my hands.

A Shapely Celebration

Shape Centers

Arrange your room with several centers for the children to experience on the final day of your *Shapes* unit. Choose activities from the list below that you have not already completed with your children or try some of them again for a review.

Center Activities

- Make a big book (page 39)

- Play the Math Shape Up games (page 43)

- Play the Bean-Bag Shape Toss game (page 63)

- Make a Shape Mobile (pages 64 and 65)

- Make a Fishy Windsock (pages 66 and 67)

Go On a Shape Walk

Take your children on a walk around the school grounds. Ask them to try to identify shapes in the objects they see. (This is a good way to assess your children's knowledge of shapes and to determine whether or not skills have improved through using the information in this unit.)

Sweet Treats

Serve a variety of shape treats.

- Shape Face Creations (page 23)

- Crackers and Cheese (page 23)

- English Muffin Pizza (page 24)

- Cookie-Cutter Sandwiches (page 24)

- Rabbit Snacks (page 61)

- Fish in the Ocean (page 62)

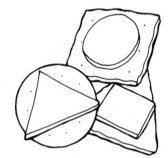

Shape-Book Sharing

Once again, read all four of the literature titles featured in this book to your children. Invite them to tell each other which books were their favorites and why. If appropriate, encourage them to read the books to each other in small groups.

Awards

Present your children with Shape Awards (page 77) to acknowledge their hard work during the *Shapes* unit.

Bulletin-board Ideas

Can You Sort the Shapes?

This interactive bulletin board display gives your children the opportunity to match identical shapes. Staple brightly colored paper for a background. Then cut out and staple seven large construction-paper pockets to the board. On each pocket, draw or attach a different shape. Place a stack of construction-paper cutout shapes (several of each shape) near the bulletin board. To interact with the display, a child places each shape into the pocket with the corresponding shape on it.

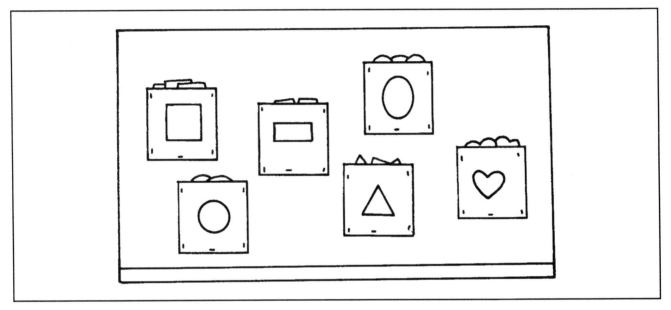

Ocean Shapes

Create an ocean setting by first attaching blue butcher paper to the bulletin board background. Then staple strips of green crepe-paper streamers to the board for seaweed. Cut out a variety of shapes in assorted colors and decorate them to look like sea creatures. Attach them to the display. Encourage your children to search for the creatures and identify the shape(s) of each.

Shapes Online

Children's Television Workshop

www.ctw.org/home/content/0,2946,,FF.html

CTW provides numerous resources for families with preschoolers. Here you'll find a Parents' Toolbox, Family Web Fun, Preschool Playground, Sesame Street Central, and Activity Time. Click on the area of your choice to reveal motivating activities.

Cozy Corner for Kids

www.meginc.com/newkids/preschool.html

This Web site contains a long list of links to activities, Web sites, and downloads on a variety of subjects, including math, literature, science, and art.

Disney.Com

disney.go.com/home/homepage/today/html/index.html

You'll find a wealth of kid-friendly activities at this entertaining Web site, including crafts, games, recipes, and activities. Enter the word "shapes" in the search window to find activities specifically related to your theme.

Early Childhood: Math

members.tripod.com/~Patricia_F/mathscience.html

After accessing this Web site, scroll down for a list of shape activities. You'll also find simple activities related to other math topics for young children.

Free Worksheets—Ages 4 to 6

www.freeworksheets.com/sub_cat1.asp?cat=Ages4to6

This site provides a large selection of printable worksheets for preschoolers about shapes, colors, counting, letters, and numbers.

Funschool.Com

www.funschool.com

Access this site to find a multitude of activities for preschoolers and older children. Click on *Preschool* and then *More Games* to find a fun online game about shapes.

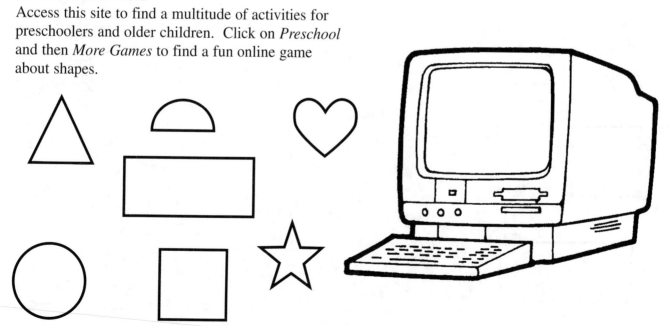

Shapes Online *(cont.)*

Kid's Domain Online Games
www.kidsdomain.com/games/online.html
You will find online games for kids, including games about shape matching, the alphabet, and drawing.

KinderArt Littles: Early Childhood Activities
www.bconnex.net/~jarea/litles.htm
This site provides a variety of preschool activities, including ABCs, art, cooperation, play, music, and more. Click on the search link at the bottom of the page and enter "shapes" to find preschool shape activities.

L'il Fingers
www.lil-fingers.com
Entertaining online storybooks for young children are available at this Web site. Click to find stories about colors, shapes, and making faces. The shape games show children how shapes are drawn.

Parent's Activity Guide: Shape Recognition
www.ctw.org/preschool/guide/skill/0,1173,3,00.html
This site provides ideas for encouraging shape recognition at home. This is a useful resource to encourage parents to work with their children at home.

Preschool Playground
www.ctw.org/preschool/guide/
Accessing this Web site reveals numerous links to games related to reading, math, thinking skills, social studies, and health. You'll find a shape game in the math section.

A World of Kindergartens
www.iup.edu/~njyost/KHI/KHI.htmlx
This online community encourages early-childhood educators to exchange ideas, ask questions, and obtain resources and activities.

Parent Page

Dear Parents,

Your child is learning about shapes. There are many ways that you can reinforce this skill at home. Have fun with your child as you try some of the activities listed below!

- Make sugar cookies using cookie cutters in assorted shapes.
- Make shapes using molding dough or clay.
- Look for shapes around the house and play, "I Spy!"
- Discuss the shapes of foods on a dinner plate.
- Look in the mirror. What shapes do you see on your face?
- Find shapes in your backyard.
- Use a cookie cutter to make sandwiches in different shapes.
- Talk about your favorite shape.
- Look for foods in the refrigerator that are shaped like circles.
- Make shape patterns using assorted shapes of crackers.
- Make finger paintings of shapes using edible pudding on a paper plate.
- Are there more circles, squares, or triangles in your house?
- March in a circle and sing a favorite song.
- Practice drawing shapes with crayons or markers.
- Draw a picture using only squares.
- Fill a bowl with salt or sand. Draw shapes in it.
- Sort toys in groups according to their shape.
- Cut out shapes and arrange them in a path on the floor. Walk on the path as you name each shape.
- Cut out paper shapes and tape them onto your refrigerator door. Name three shapes each time you pass by.

Thanks for your support. I know that the more activities you and your child do together, the more "in shape" he/she will be!

Sincerely,

Shape Patterns

Shape Patterns *(cont.)*

Awards

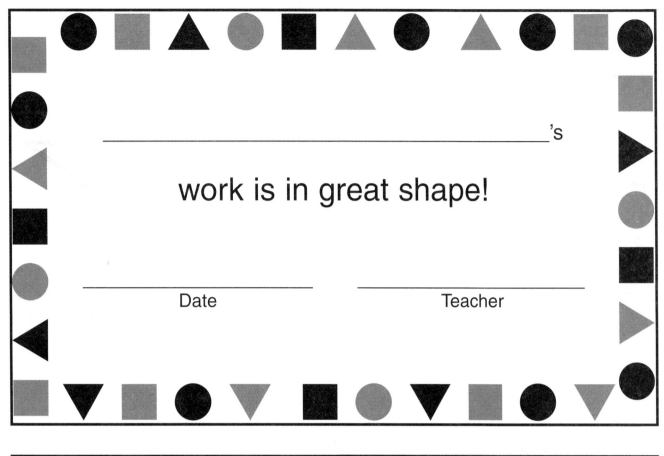

_____'s

work is in great shape!

_____
Date

_____
Teacher

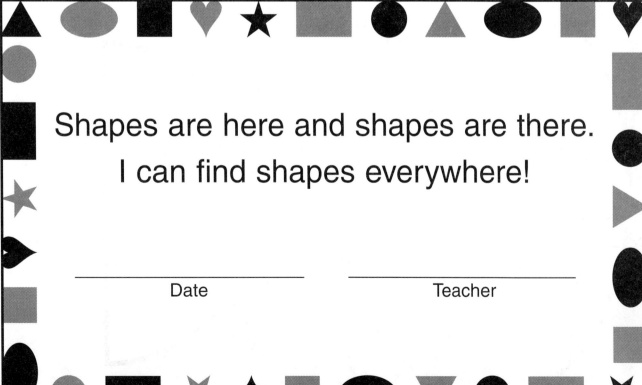

Shapes are here and shapes are there.
I can find shapes everywhere!

_____
Date

_____
Teacher

Annotated Software

Fisher-Price: Ready for Preschool
by Knowledge Adventure, Inc.

This three-level program takes place at a circus. It focuses on a variety of preschool skills in the areas of math and language. Appropriate for ages 2–4. Available for Windows and Macintosh.

James Discovers Math
by Brøderbund

This delightful animated program offers interactive practice with reasoning, problem solving, measurement, geometry, numeration, and computation. Appropriate for ages 5–9. Available for Windows and Macintosh.

JumpStart Math for First Graders
by Knowledge Adventure, Inc.

Frankie the Dog takes children on a math adventure through a large backyard. Many skills are featured, including counting money, telling time, weights and measures, and geometry. Appropriate for ages 5–7. Available for Windows and Macintosh.

Math Blaster 4–6
by Knowledge Adventure, Inc.

Join Blasternaut and friends for energetic practice with addition, subtraction, colors, counting, estimation, patterns, and shapes. Ten space activities with three levels of difficulty make this program a "blast" for kids. Appropriate for ages 4–6. Available for Windows and Macintosh.

Piggy in Numberland
by Legacy Interactive

Children journey to enchanted castles, hidden playgrounds, and secret houses where they learn numbers, counting, addition, subtraction, counting money, patterns, spatial relationships, and shapes. Appropriate for ages 4–7. Available for Windows only.

Sesame Street Numbers
by Children's Television Workshop

This program provides eight learning activities for learning numbers and number concepts. Activities include learning games, Sesame Street songs, and storybooks. Featured skills include counting, addition, subtraction, near/far, and classification. Appropriate for ages 3–6. Available for Windows and Macintosh.

Annotated Bibliography

Barney's Book of Shapes
by Darren McKee (Barney Publishing, 1998)
Barney has many shape friends. This interactive book introduces children to Rhonda the Rectangle, Cecil the Circle, and more.

Beach Ball
by Peter Sis (Greenwillow, 1998)
A child follows a beach ball while walking along a beach. The illustrations encourage children to search for shapes, colors, and letters.

Bear in a Square
by Stella Blackstone (Barefoot Books, 1998)
Your children will enjoy searching this book's illustrations for a variety of shapes.

Circle Dogs
by Kevin Henkes (Greenwillow, 1998)
Two circle dogs live in a big square house. They dig circle holes and eat circle snacks. Bold illustrations will intrigue young children.

Color Zoo
by Lois Ehlert (HarperCollins, 1997)
This die-cut picture book uses shapes to transform pictures into a variety of familiar animals.

Cookie Shapes
by John Fosberg (Little Saint Simons Island, 1997)
Young children learn about squares, circles, ovals, and other shapes in this book featuring cookies, cookies, and more cookies.

Exploring Shapes
by Andrew King (Copper Beech Books, 1998)
Interactive math projects provide discovery experiences with shapes.

The Greedy Triangle
by Marilyn Burns (Scholastic Trade, 1995)
A little triangle is tired of being a triangle. He decides to change his shape by becoming a series of different shapes. He finally decides that being a triangle is the best shape to be.

The Missing Piece
by Shel Silverstein (HarperCollins, 1976)
A circle rolls across the countryside in search of a missing triangular piece. It encounters many shapes along the way until it finds the one that fits.

The Patchwork Quilt
by Valerie Flournoy (EP Dutton, 1985)
A young girl watches her grandmother make a quilt from pieces of fabric cut from the clothes of family members.

Annotated Bibliography (cont.)

The Shape Detectives
by Angela Santomero (Simon Spotlight, 1998)
Your children will enjoy searching through the house of Blue and Steve, looking for a variety of shapes.

The Shape of Things
by Dayle Ann Dodds (Demco Media, 1996)
This creatively illustrated book shows children that shapes can be found all around us.

The Silly Story of Goldilocks and the Three Squares
by Grace MacCarone (Cartwheel, 1996)
This familiar story has a shapely twist as Goldilocks enters a pentagon house with geometric furniture. Will she escape before the three Squares come home?

So Many Circles, So Many Squares
by Tana Hoban (Greenwillow, 1998)
This wordless picture book displays photographs of circle- and square-shaped objects in the city.

Spirals, Curves, Fanshapes and Lines
by Tana Hoban (Greenwillow, 1992)
Spirals, curves, fanshapes, and lines are everywhere. Tana Hoban's photographs artistically display these shapes in everyday life.

Ten Black Dots
by Donald Crews (Mulberry Books, 1995)
This creative book uses black dots to represent the sun, a fox's eyes, and many more familiar objects. The rhyming text will have your children reading along as you count from one to ten.

Three Pigs, One Wolf, and Seven Magic Shapes
by Grace MacCarone (Scholastic, 1998)
This familiar tale with a twist introduces your children to shapes and tangrams.